Old Hawor

by
Ann Dinsdale

One of the earliest known images of Haworth,
reproduced from *The Christian Miscellany*, January 1858.

Published by Hendon Publishing Co.
Printed by Fretwell Print and Design Ltd, Keighley, West Yorkshire BD21 1PZ

Plan of Haworth, surveyed by J.O. Brierly for the newly established Haworth Local Board of Health, 1853.

Old Haworth

•••'heaven did not seem to be my home; and I broke my heart with weeping to come back to earth; and the angels were so angry that they flung me out, into the middle of the heath on the top of Wuthering Heights; where I woke sobbing for joy.' Emily Brontë, *Wuthering Heights* (1847).

Millions have been drawn to Haworth and the surrounding moors by the power of the Brontë novels. The Brontës were firmly rooted in Haworth and the sad story of their lives exerts as much fascination as their fiction. Elizabeth Gaskell's romanticized biography, published two years after Charlotte's death, has drawn people from all over the world to the grim moorland village which in the mid-nineteenth century was the home of Charlotte (1816-1855), Emily (1818-1848) and Anne (1820-1849) Brontë, and where they wrote some of the greatest novels in the English language.

The Brontës came to Haworth in 1820, when the youngest, Anne, was still a babe-in-arms. Haworth Parsonage remained the family's home for the rest of their lives, and the wild Yorkshire landscape had a profound influence on their writing. At that time a third of Haworth's rough-hewn population was employed in the textile industry, often working in their own homes combing wool for the mills. The poor living conditions resulted in a high mortality rate, but when Mrs Brontë died within eighteen months of the family's arrival there, it was cancer that killed her. The two eldest daughters, Maria and Elizabeth, died from tuberculosis in 1825 aged eleven and ten years. Looking out from the Parsonage windows, the surviving members of the family were perpetually confronted by the sight of the melancholy graveyard and their father's church, an ever-present reminder of their dead mother and sisters laid in the vault below.

For the next few years the three surviving sisters and their brother Branwell remained at home together, creating a rich imaginary world, chronicled in tiny books with minuscule handwriting to deter the prying eyes of the Parsonage adults. Eventually the Brontës had to leave the Parsonage and earn their living as teachers or governesses. They made use of their own experience and memories of actual places in their writings, but like all artists they were selective in their use of descriptive detail. The schools and private houses where Charlotte taught suggested the settings for her most famous novels, *Jane Eyre* (1847) and *Villette* (1853). Governess life provided Anne with 'some very unpleasant and undreamt of experience of human nature', which found its way into her novels *Agnes Grey* (1847) and *The Tenant of Wildfell Hall* (1848). Emily craved an isolated life at the Parsonage where she produced her only novel, *Wuthering Heights* (1847).

Patrick Brontë outlived all his gifted family. By 1849 Branwell, Emily and Anne had all died in rapid succession, their deaths followed six years later by that of Charlotte, newly married and in the early stages of pregnancy. Although tragic, the Brontës' early deaths were not particularly remarkable in a village where forty-one per cent of the children born died before reaching the age of six. The gradual introduction of health reforms in Haworth, for which Patrick Brontë campaigned, came too late to benefit his own family.

Patrick Brontë died aged eighty-four in 1861. The years since his death have seen many changes in Haworth, and the church where he preached for forty-one years has been demolished and rebuilt. Patrick's successor, the Reverend John Wade, outraged many Brontë enthusiasts when he made alterations to the Parsonage and added a large gabled wing to create more space for his own family. The Parsonage served as home to three more incumbents after Wade until it was acquired by the Brontë Society and opened as a museum in 1928. Nowadays the Brontë Parsonage Museum houses the world's largest collection of Brontëana, and as a literary shrine, is second only to Shakespeare's home at Stratford.

It became a fixed idea from early on that the literary tourist could physically travel through the landscapes of the Brontës' imaginations. A ruined old farmhouse called Top Withens, high on the moors above Haworth, has entered Brontë mythology as the site of Wuthering Heights in Emily's novel. Top Withens never resembled the Heights, but its dramatic moorland setting fits the bill perfectly. Haworth remains an interesting place with or without the Brontës, but the visitor lured by its literary associations should do as the Brontës themselves did: turn away from the village and head towards the moors, described so hauntingly by Charlotte after her sisters' deaths:

'. . . when I go out there alone everything reminds me of the times when others were with me, and then the moors seem a wilderness, featureless, solitary, saddening. My sister Emily had a particular love for them, and there is not a knoll of heather, not a branch of fern, not a young bilberry leaf, not a fluttering lark or linnet, but reminds me of her. The distant prospects were Anne's delight, and when I look round she is in the blue tints, the pale mists, the waves and shadows of the horizon. In the hill-country silence their poetry comes by lines and stanzas into my mind: once I loved it; now I dare not read it . . .'

1/ Haworth Old Church and Parsonage c.1860. The graveyard was extended into the field in the foreground in 1856, and all too soon filled with graves.

2/ 'Right before the traveller on this road rises Haworth village; he can see it for two miles before he arrives, for it is situated on the side of a pretty steep hill, with a background of dun and purple moors, rising and sweeping away yet higher than the church, which is built at the very summit of the long narrow street.' Elizabeth Gaskell, *The Life of Charlotte Brontë* (1857).

3/ A late 1880s view of Haworth Brow. A great deal of terraced housing has since been built here. In the mid-nineteenth century most of Haworth's population worked in their own homes combing wool for the mills. The quarries also offered employment to large numbers of men (there are two just visible in this photograph). Baptist and Wesleyan chapels flourished, and along with the church, provided much of the community's social life. The Butterfield Memorial Chapel can be seen off to the right here, with the Clarendon Brewery (later Parker's Brewery) above.

4/ Haworth Old Hall was probably built in the late sixteenth or early seventeenth century, possibly by the then Lord of Haworth Manor, Martin Birkhead, or his son Nathaniel. In 1618 it was acquired by the Scotts of Oxenhope, and then descended through marriage to the Ramsden family of Greetland (they later took the name Hawksworth), who owned the Hall as well as a large part of Haworth until the mid-eighteenth century. In 1749 the whole property was bought by their friends, the Emmots of Lancashire. Although often known as Emmot Hall, the Emmots never occupied it, but let it out as a farm, sometimes called Hall Farm. Descendants of the Emmots continued to own it well into the twentieth century.

5/ A scene of celebration during the First World War. Brontë interests seem to have continued in Haworth quite undampened by the Great War. The centenary of Charlotte Brontë's birth was celebrated in June 1916 and attracted a 'vast crowd'. Many walked on the moors and to the Brontë waterfall. At that time the famous Branwell Brontë chair from the Black Bull belonged to William Sugden, a former landlord, who had left it in the care of his sister and her husband, Mr and Mrs Parker. They decided to exhibit the chair to passers-by their home in West Lane and collected for the Red Cross. This 'happy idea' raised over three pounds for the Keighley War Hospital Depot.

6/ A view of the lower section of Main Street, dating from around 1910. The tall building on the left is the former Co-op, while the building next door belonged to West Parker, umbrella maker. Also seen in this photograph is a rather wonderful gas lamp. The scheme for lighting Haworth's streets by gas was initiated by the Local Board of Health in 1864.

7/ In 1850 there were no sewers in Haworth and drainage ran in open channels down the Main Street. Babbage's 1850 report paints a grim picture of a village littered with stagnant pools and midden heaps, in which the refuse of slaughter houses and 'night soil' was left to decompose until it was washed away down the street. In this photograph dating from the late 1870s, the shop in the foreground is that of James Ogden, a linen draper, and the white cottages in the centre (no longer standing) were occupied by James Whitham, a carrier, and Simeon Townend, a cabinet maker. The front of the Three Graces Lodge can be seen in the distance.

8/ A view looking towards the top of Butt Lane and Main Street, with the Fleece in the centre. The small wooden building on stilts at the top of Butt Lane is said to have been John Toothill's barber's shop, patronized by the Revd. Patrick Brontë. The farm buildings were used by Hiram Hey to store his horse-drawn carts and hearse.

9/ In the census for 1891, Hiram Hey was described as a forty-four year old farmer and cab proprietor living at 12 Main Street with his wife Ann and son Willie, a 'cab proprietor's assistant'. At the time of his death in 1902, Hey was described as a 'cab proprietor and mineral manufacturer' of 'Bull Lane', Haworth. This could be a mis-print for Butt Lane, where Hey's premises are shown in this photograph taken at about the same period.

10/ In the 1891 census, Manasseh Hollindrake of Main Street was described as a master draper. His son Charles Edwin was an assistant draper and his daughter Sarah Mary was a milliner. Manasseh had been born in Silsden, but his wife and children were all born in Haworth. Manasseh died in 1919 and is buried in Haworth churchyard with his wife Mary and four infant sons. A good example of a draper's advertising in the early 1900s is provided by another Haworth draper, J.P. Knight, 'The People's Clothier', of 27 Mill Hey, who advertised 'All the Latest Novelties in Hats, Caps, Collars and Fronts, and oh! What Neckties!!' He then launched into verse:

> There are friendship's ties and business ties,
> And family ties from birth,
> But you'll find the ties we advertise
> Are the prettiest ties on earth.

11/ In 1836 Branwell Brontë was initiated into the Masonic Lodge of the Three Graces. Throughout the period of Branwell's membership, the Lodge meetings took place in a private house (seen to the right of this photograph with a ladder against it) at Newell Hill, which has since become known as Lodge Street. Across from the Masonic building was the home of William Wood (1808-1889), the Haworth joiner. In his workshop on the second floor, Wood made several articles of furniture for the Brontës, including their coffins. His aunt was Tabitha Aykroyd, who for thirty years was a servant at the Parsonage. In 1836 Wood and Tabitha jointly purchased three cottages in Lodge Street, and it was possibly to one of these that Tabitha eventually retired.

12/ Haworth's steep Main Street is cobbled with wide stone setts, which Elizabeth Gaskell tells us were intended 'to give a better hold to the horses' feet; and, even with this help, they seem in constant danger of slipping backwards.' In this photograph the Black Bull can be seen at the very top of the street.

13/ Elizabeth Gaskell claimed that Branwell Brontë's conversational skills earned him 'the undesirable distinction of having his company recommended by the landlord of the Black Bull to any chance traveller who might happen to feel solitary or dull over his liquor.' Despite the fact that alcoholism contributed to Branwell's death at the age of thirty-one, it was estimated that the consumption of beer and spirits in Haworth was very much below the average, the equivalent of about one-ninth of a pint per person daily.

14/ The wedding of Gertrude Maude Smith and Edwin Earnshaw took place in Haworth in July 1903. Gertrude had been born in Haworth on 15 July 1878 and Edwin was a Cullingworth man, born on 23 July 1875. The finery of the wedding party is contrasted with the mill shawls and flat caps of the bystanders.

15/ In 1850 there were seven public houses operating in Haworth, mainly within a stone's throw of the Church. In this photograph the Cross Inn can be seen on the right while the Old White Lion faces down the street. Haworth has seen many attempts over the years to cash in on the Brontë name: the Brontë Café can be seen on the right, and in 1889 a collection of Brontë relics was exhibited in the tall building opposite. At that time the building served as a temperance tea room, run by Francis and Robinson Brown, cousins of Martha Brown (1828-1880), a former servant at the Parsonage.

16/ Some of Haworth's poorest inhabitants lived in this area known as 'Brandy Row'. The area probably took its name from the fact that it was approached through a courtyard adjoining the premises of a wine and spirits merchant. The courtyard in turn was entered through a stone archway at the top of Main Street, and the whole area was also known as 'Gaugers Croft' on account of the gaugers or excise men who made visits to check on the spirits brought into the warehouses.

17/ In the 1850 report into Haworth's sanitary conditions it was stated that 'one of the most striking features to be met with in an examination of Haworth, is the very small number of privies, being only 1 to every $4^1/2$ houses.' Improvements reached Brandy Row slowly, and over a hundred years later in 1964, a report published by the Civic Trust claimed the houses were 'technically unfit', with one block having '. . . only one exterior lavatory for three houses.' Brandy Row, demolished in the 1960s, is shown here with the back of Main Street in the distance.

18/ The Brontë Society, founded in 1893, opened its first Brontë museum two years later on the upper floor of the Yorkshire Penny Bank, now the Tourist Information Centre, at the top of Haworth's Main Street. The Museum remained here for thirty-three years.

19/ The crowded interior of the Brontë Society's first museum in Haworth, before the Parsonage was acquired in 1928. The plaster medallion portrait of Branwell Brontë can be seen on the far wall, with drawings and paintings by his sisters on the left.

20/ In his 1850 report, Babbage condemned the Haworth practice of covering graves with large flat stones which prevented the access of air to the ground and the growth of plants which would assist decomposition. The trees we see in the graveyard today were planted in 1864 as a result of his report.

21/ Patrick Brontë was Perpetual Curate of Haworth Church from 1820 until his death in 1861. With the exception of the tower, the building was demolished in 1879 and rebuilt on the same site. The Old Church had a double-gabled roof, the outline of which can still be seen on the tower.

22/ The interior of Haworth Old Church, where Charlotte Brontë married the Reverend Arthur Bell Nicholls, her father's curate, on 29 June 1854. It was said that on her wedding day Charlotte looked 'like a snowdrop', in her white muslin dress and bonnet trimmed with green leaves.

23/ A plaque inside Haworth Church records the deaths of the Brontë family, who with the exception of Anne, were buried in a vault beneath the church floor. Anne died at Scarborough, and is buried there in the churchyard of St. Mary's.

24/ This photograph shows the Sunday school with the sexton's house adjoining. Prior to his marriage to Charlotte, the Curate, Arthur Bell Nicholls, lodged here with the Brown family.

25/ The National Church Sunday school was built in 1832. The Brontës taught here, with Branwell being remembered amongst his young scholars chiefly for his bad temper. It was here that Charlotte and Arthur Bell Nicholls entertained the scholars and Sunday school teachers to supper following their marriage in 1854. In all, five hundred people attended, and according to Charlotte, 'They seemed to enjoy it much . . .'

26/ The earliest known image of Haworth Parsonage, an ambrotype which is believed to date from the 1850s. The photograph has been taken from the tower of the old church.

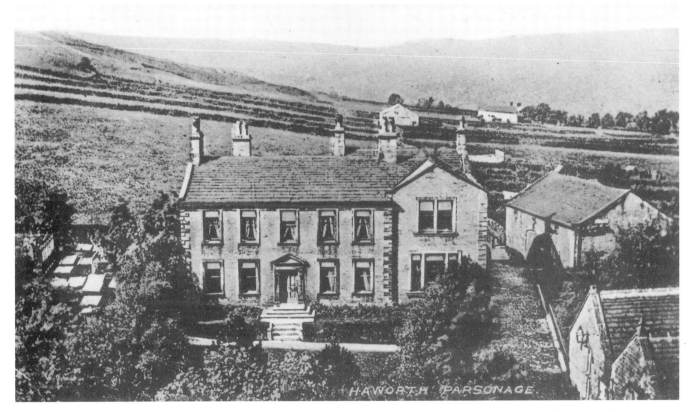

27/ After Patrick Brontë's death in 1861 Haworth Parsonage became the home of the Revd. John Wade, who added the new wing in the 1870s. The barn, which was used as a stonemason's workshop in the Brontës' time, was demolished in 1903. This photograph has also been taken from the church tower, but by this time a new section had been added to incorporate the clock, making the tower higher.

28/ On 4 August 1928, over sixty years after the death of the last member of the Brontë family, thousands gathered to see the official opening of their former home as the Brontë Parsonage Museum.

29/ Haworth Parsonage was purchased by Sir James Roberts, a local boy made good. In handing over the title deeds to the Brontë Society in 1928 he told the assembled crowd: 'It is to me a somewhat melancholy reflection that I am one of the fast narrowing circle of Haworth veterans who remember the Parsonage family . . .'

Haworth Church Sunday School.

FOUNDATION STONE OF NEW SCHOOL

LAID BY

George Merrall, Esq., May 23rd, 1903.

(Law House)

30/ The new Haworth Church Sunday School formerly stood on the site of the car park, opposite the Brontë Parsonage Museum. The building was the scene of many Sunday school events and dramatic productions, but was demolished in the 1960s when dry rot took hold.

31/ Haworth's most famous incumbent is usually assumed to be Patrick Brontë, but the village had already attracted fame a century before Patrick's arrival, under the ministry of the Revd. William Grimshaw (1708-1763), a leader of the eighteenth-century Evangelical Revival. In 1742 when Grimshaw was appointed to Haworth, the Parsonage had not yet been built and Grimshaw lived in this old farmhouse, Sowdens, on the edge of the moors. Colourful tales abound of him driving his parishioners from public house to church brandishing a horsewhip. His sudden death in 1763 robbed the Evangelicals of a leading light.

32/ An early twentieth-century view of Changegate, formerly known as 'The Ginnel'. The wooden building to the right was John Wood's Joiner's shop. The cottages behind were part of Well Street, demolished in the 1960s. The row of cottages on the left was known as 'Spout Stones'.

TOWNEND

33/ Town End, a beautifully restored seventeenth-century farmhouse, was the home of the Binns family. The house stands on Back Lane (North Street in modern Haworth). The cart standing outside the barn is a reminder that the Binns family worked as carriers besides farming Town End, and they also provided horses to draw the fire engine which was housed across North Street in the old lock-up at the end of Gibb Lane.

34/ An early twentieth-century photograph showing a horse and cart delivering groceries, taken on Changegate at the top of Lord Lane.

35/ The manor house at Cook Gate was built in the eighteenth century, and is very similar in appearance to Haworth Parsonage. At one time it was the home of Amos Ingham (1827-1889), the Haworth doctor who attended Charlotte Brontë in the last few months of her life, and who in 1870 built Ashmount, another fine house in Haworth.

36/ This small stone bridge, which spans South Dean Beck, is known as the 'Brontë Bridge'. Close to the Brontë Waterfall, it is said to have been a favourite haunt of the Brontës. This bridge carried one of a number of tracks and footpaths which served the farms of the Sladen and South Dean valleys. Much of this pathway system was disrupted by the building of Lower Laithe Reservoir, though traces of these paths can still be seen on the valley sides on the way to the 'Brontë Bridge'.

MISS LILY COVE VICTIM OF PARACHUTE ACCIDENT, AT HOWARTH.

AND CAPT BIDMEAD. HER EMPLOYER.

WHITE & PROCTER, PHOTO KEIGHLEY

37/ In June 1906, a young aeronaut, Miss Lily Cove, was hired as the star attraction of the Haworth Gala. It was planned that Lily would make a balloon ascent from the Gala field (now the cricket field on West Lane), and descend by parachute further up the Worth Valley. On the day of the Gala several thousand people were disappointed when the balloon failed to rise, and the attempt was re-scheduled for the following Monday evening. This time Lily was able to make her ascent without problems, but just ten minutes later she plummeted to her death in a field close to Ponden Reservoir. An inquest failed to discover why Lily became detached from her parachute. Her gravestone in the cemetery on the edge of Haworth moor was raised by public subscription, and carries a replica of the balloon and parachute she used.

38/ The moors are dotted with the ruins of old farmhouses where the hardy few eked out a living from subsistence farming. The Water Board depopulated many of these farms in an attempt to avoid sewage seepage into the Worth Valley reservoirs.

39/ Lower Laithe farm was demolished when the Smith Bank area was flooded during the construction of the reservoir, 1914-1925.

40/ The hamlet of Smith Bank would have been familiar to the Brontë family. Much of this area was flooded during the construction of Lower Laithe Reservoir, completed in 1925. The track seen here is Waterhead Lane, which was the Oxenhope-Stanbury route before the construction of the reservoir, when it was replaced by the new road over the dam.

41/ Work began on the construction of Lower Laithe Reservoir in 1914, but was delayed by the intervention of the war. This photograph shows the puddle trench stretching across the valley. Just beyond the end of the puddle trench is the site office, with Intake Farm above. Penistone Hill can be seen in the distance.

42/ Top Withens farm lies about four miles from Haworth Parsonage. It has often been associated with *Wuthering Heights*, and though it is possible that Emily Brontë had the moorland setting of Withens in mind when she wrote her novel, the old, now-ruined farmhouse bears no similarity to the house she described.

43/ Throughout the nineteenth-century Top Withens was occupied by members of the Sunderland family, some of whom are buried in the churchyard at Haworth. The last recorded occupant was Ernest Roddy, a poultry farmer, in 1926.

44/ A view of Haworth Old Church taken before its demolition in 1879. The tower is all that remains of the original building, and in this photograph a new section has been added to incorporate a clock. This was one of a number of raisings of the tower which led Keighley people to say that the Haworth folk 'mucked the tower to mak it grow.'